2. **Chapter 1: The Power of Mindset**

- Creating a mindset that fosters wealth.

Creating a wealth mindset is a vital step towards achieving financial freedom. It involves changing how you think about money and wealth, shifting from a scarcity mindset to an abundance mindset, and cultivating habits that lead to wealth creation. Here are some steps you can take to create a wealth mindset:

1. **Believe in Abundance**: Wealth and abundance are not finite. There's enough for everyone. Believe that you can create wealth and be open to opportunities that come your way.

2. **Set Clear Financial Goals**: What does financial freedom look like for you? Define this clearly and set specific, measurable, achievable, realistic, and timely (SMART) financial goals.

3. **Education and Learning**: Invest in financial education. Read books, listen to podcasts, or take courses on personal finance and wealth creation. Knowledge is the foundation of wealth.

4. **Practice Gratitude**: Be grateful for what you have, even as you strive for more. Gratitude fosters positivity and openness to receive more.

5. **Invest Wisely**: Understand the power of investments over just savings. Stocks, bonds, real estate, or starting your own business can generate passive income and increase your wealth over time.

6. **Live Below Your Means**: Avoid the trap of lifestyle inflation. As your income increases, keep your expenses constant or only slightly increased.

7. **Surround Yourself with Positive Influences**: They say you're the average of the five people you spend the most time with. Surround yourself with people who inspire you, challenge you, and motivate you towards wealth creation.

I0436626

8. **Embrace Failure as a Learning Opportunity**: Failure is not the opposite of success; it's part of the journey to success. Each failure brings you one step closer to your goals.

9. **Consistently Practice Wealth-Attracting Habits**: Consistency is key. Make wealth-attracting habits like saving, investing, and continuous learning part of your daily routine.

- Understanding the importance of confidence, resilience, and a growth mindset.

Understanding the importance of confidence, resilience, and a growth mindset is crucial for personal and professional development. These traits not only affect how we approach challenges and opportunities, but they also play a significant role in our overall happiness and satisfaction in life.

1. **Confidence**: Confidence is about trusting in your abilities, qualities, and judgment. When you are confident, you're not afraid to take on challenges, express your thoughts, and stand up for what you believe in. It also helps you make decisions more effectively and take calculated risks that can lead to significant rewards. Confidence is attractive to others as well - it can help you establish strong relationships, both personally and professionally.

2. **Resilience**: Resilience is the ability to recover quickly from difficulties; it's about being able to bounce back after experiencing adversity. Life is full of challenges, but resilient people view these challenges as opportunities to grow and learn. They don't let failure define them; instead, they use it as a stepping stone to success. Resilience also helps you maintain a positive outlook and manage stress effectively, which is crucial for mental health.

3. **Growth Mindset**: A growth mindset is the belief that abilities and intelligence can be developed through dedication and hard work. People with a growth mindset are always eager to learn and improve. They are not afraid of making mistakes, as they see them as

opportunities to learn. They embrace challenges, persist in the face of setbacks, and understand that effort is the path to

- Strategies to overcome fear and doubts.

Overcoming fear and doubts is an essential part of personal growth and achieving success. Here are some strategies that can help:

1. **Understand Your Fear**: Identify what exactly you're afraid of. Is it failure, rejection, uncertainty, or something else? Understanding your fear is the first step in overcoming it.

2. **Positive Affirmations**: Use positive affirmations to counteract negative thoughts and self-doubt. Tell yourself you are capable, strong, and worthy. This can help shift your mindset and boost your self-confidence.

3. **Set Realistic Goals**: Setting achievable goals can give you something to work towards and help mitigate feelings of fear and doubt. It's crucial to break down large goals into smaller, manageable steps.

4. **Visualize Success**: Visualization is a powerful tool. Imagine yourself successfully overcoming your fear or doubt. This can help to make the outcome seem more attainable.

5. **Practice Mindfulness and Meditation**: These techniques can help reduce anxiety and stress, making it easier to deal with fear and doubt. They encourage a focus on the present moment, rather than worrying about the future.

6. **Seek Support**: Don't hesitate to seek help from friends, family, or professionals. They can provide advice, encouragement, and a different perspective.

7. **Embrace Failure**: Understand that failure is a part of life and it's often where we learn the most. Instead of fearing failure, try to see it as an opportunity for growth and learning.

Remember, it's perfectly normal to have fears and doubts. What's important is not to let them control your life. With the right strategies, you can overcome them and move forward with confidence.

3. **Chapter 2: Building a Solid Financial Plan**

- Assessing your current financial status.

Assessing your current financial status is critical for planning your future and achieving your financial goals. Here are steps you can follow:

1. **Calculate Your Net Worth**: This is the difference between your assets (what you own) and liabilities (what you owe). Your assets include savings, investments, real estate, etc., while liabilities could be loans, credit card debts, etc.

2. **Analyze Your Income**: Determine your total income. This includes your salary, dividends, rental income, etc. It's also good to understand the stability of your income.

3. **Track Your Expenses**: Record all your expenses, including bills, groceries, rent, entertainment, etc. This will give you a clear picture of where your money is going and help identify areas where you can cut back.

4. **Evaluate Your Savings**: Look at how much you're saving each month, and consider if it's enough to meet your future goals. A general rule is to save at least 20% of your income.

5. **Review Your Debt**: Evaluate your current debt situation. High-interest debt, like credit card debt, should be paid off as quickly as possible.

6. **Check Your Credit Score**: Your credit score is a measure of your financial health and creditworthiness. It's important to ensure you have a good credit score for future loans or credit needs.

7. **Retirement Planning**: Assess your current retirement savings and whether they are on track to meet your retirement goals.

8. **Insurance Coverage**: Review your insurance policies to ensure you have adequate coverage for health, life, and property.

9. **Investment Portfolio**: Review your investments to see if they align with your risk tolerance and financial goals.

This assessment should provide a comprehensive overview of your financial status. It's a good practice to do this regularly to stay on top of your financial health and make necessary adjustments.

- **Setting financial goals and creating a realistic plan.**

Setting financial goals and creating a realistic plan requires thoughtful consideration and discipline. Here is a step-by-step guide:

1. **Define Your Goals**: Start by identifying what you want to achieve. Your goals could be short-term (like saving for a vacation), medium-term (like saving for a down payment on a house), or long-term (like saving for retirement).

2. **Prioritize Your Goals**: Not all goals are created equal. Prioritize your goals based on their importance and urgency. This will help you focus your resources effectively.

3. **Quantify Your Goals**: Assign a specific dollar amount to each goal. This will make it easier to track your progress and stay motivated.

4. **Set a Timeline**: Decide by when you want to achieve each goal. This will help you determine how much you need to save or invest each month.

5. **Create a Budget**: Track your income and expenses to understand where your money is going. This will help you identify areas where you can cut back and save more towards your goals.

6. **Consider Investments**: Depending on your goals and timeline, investing could help grow your money faster. It's important to understand the risks involved and consider seeking advice from a financial advisor if you're new to investing.

7. **Automate Savings**: Consider setting up automatic transfers to your savings or investment accounts. This ensures you're consistently contributing towards your goals.

8. **Regularly Review and Adjust Your Plan**: Your financial situation and goals may change over time. Regularly reviewing and adjusting your plan will keep you on track.

9. **Build an Emergency Fund**: Life is unpredictable. It's advisable to keep 3-6 months of living expenses in a readily

- Importance of budgeting and saving.

Budgeting and saving are two crucial elements of sound financial management. Here is why they are so important:

1. **Control Over Your Money**: A budget provides a roadmap for your money. It helps you understand where your money is going, enabling you to make informed decisions about spending and saving. This level of control helps prevent overspending and ensures you're not caught off guard by unexpected expenses.

2. **Helps Achieve Financial Goals**: Whether it's buying a new car, going for a vacation, or saving for retirement, all financial goals require savings. A budget helps you plan your savings effectively, ensuring you stay on track to achieve your goals.

3. **Prevents Debt**: By keeping track of your income and expenses, a budget helps you live within your means. This means you're less likely to overspend and resort to credit, helping prevent debt.

4. **Emergency Preparedness**: Life can throw unexpected expenses your way, such as car repairs or medical bills. A savings cushion helps you handle these unexpected costs without going into debt.

5. **Peace of Mind**: Knowing you're in control of your finances and have a safety net of savings provides peace of mind. It reduces stress and allows you to enjoy your present life while also preparing for the future.

6. **Financial Independence**: Saving money is crucial for financial independence. Whether it's investing in opportunities, starting a business, or retiring comfortably, savings provide the capital necessary to take those steps.

In short, budgeting ensures you're making the best use of your income, and saving sets you up for a secure and comfortable future.

4.**Chapter3:Investing Wisely**

- Understanding the basics of investment.

Investment is the process of allocating money or resources to an asset or venture with the expectation of generating a profit or income over time. Here are some key concepts to understand the basics of investment:

1. **Types of Investments**: There are various types of investments, including stocks, bonds, real estate, mutual funds, exchange-traded funds (ETFs), commodities, and more. Each investment type has its own risk and return characteristics, so it's important to diversify your portfolio to manage risk.

2. **Risk and Return**: Investments inherently involve risk. Generally, higher-risk investments have the potential for higher returns, while lower-risk investments offer more stability but lower potential returns. It's important to assess your risk tolerance and investment goals to find the right balance between risk and return.

3. **Diversification**: Diversification is spreading your investments across different asset classes, industries, and regions to reduce risk. By diversifying, you can potentially minimize the impact of any single investment's performance on your overall portfolio.

4. **Time Horizon**: Your investment time horizon refers to the length of time you plan to invest before needing the funds. Longer time horizons allow for more aggressive investment strategies and the potential to ride out market fluctuations.

5. **Compounding**: Compounding is the process of earning returns not only on your initial investment but also on the accumulated returns. Over time, compounding can significantly enhance your investment gains, making it important to start investing early and consistently.

6. **Research and Due Diligence**: Before investing, it's crucial to research and understand the investment opportunity. This involves analyzing the company or asset, examining its financials, evaluating market trends, and considering any associated risks.

7. **Investment Vehicles**: There are different investment vehicles to consider, such as individual stocks, bonds, mutual funds, index funds, and more. Each has its own features, fees, and benefits, so it's important to choose the ones that align with your investment goals and risk tolerance.

8. **Monitoring and Review**: Regularly monitor your investments to stay informed about their performance. Periodic review allows you to make necessary adjustments to your portfolio based on market conditions, changes in your financial goals, or new investment opportunities.

Remember, investing involves risk, and it's important to consult with a financial advisor or do thorough research before making any investment decisions.

- Identifying the right investment opportunities.

Identifying the right investment opportunities requires careful analysis and consideration. Here are some factors to consider when evaluating investment opportunities:

1. **Goals and Risk Tolerance**: Start by defining your investment goals and risk tolerance. Are you looking for long-term growth, regular income, or capital preservation? Assess your comfort level with risk and determine the level of potential losses you can tolerate.

2. **Market Analysis**: Conduct a thorough analysis of the market or industry in which you are considering investing. Look for trends,

growth potential, and any factors that could impact the investment's performance. Consider economic indicators, market dynamics, and competitive landscape.

3. **Financial Analysis**: Evaluate the financial health and performance of the investment opportunity. Review financial statements, such as balance sheets, income statements, and cash flow statements, to assess profitability, revenue growth, debt levels, and overall financial stability.

4. **Management Team**: Assess the competence and experience of the management team behind the investment opportunity. Look for a track record of success, industry expertise, and a clear strategic vision. The management team plays a crucial role in the success of any investment.

5. **Competitive Advantage**: Identify the competitive advantage of the investment opportunity. Does it have unique features, intellectual property, or market positioning that gives it an edge over competitors? A strong competitive advantage can contribute to long-term success.

6. **Valuation**: Evaluate the investment's valuation to determine if it is reasonably priced. Consider factors such as price-to-earnings ratio, price-to-book ratio, and other valuation metrics. Compare the valuation to industry peers and historical averages.

7. **Risk Assessment**: Assess the risks associated with the investment. Consider factors such as market risk, regulatory risk, geopolitical risk, and company-specific risks. Evaluate the potential impact of these risks on the investment's performance.

8. **Diversification**: Consider how the investment opportunity fits into your overall investment portfolio. Diversification helps spread risk and can enhance overall returns. Ensure that the investment opportunity aligns with your diversification strategy.

9. **Professional Advice**: Consult with a financial advisor or investment professional who can provide guidance and expertise. They can help analyze investment opportunities, assess your

financial situation, and provide personalized recommendations based on your goals and risk tolerance.

Remember, investing involves uncertainty, and there is no guarantee of returns. It's important to conduct thorough research, stay informed about market conditions, and make informed investment decisions based on your unique circumstances and goals.

- Diversification and risk management.

Diversification and risk management are two key concepts in investing that can help mitigate risk and improve overall portfolio performance. Here's a closer look at each:

1. **Diversification**: Diversification involves spreading your investments across different asset classes (e.g., stocks, bonds, real estate), industries, regions, and even currencies. The goal is to reduce the impact of any single investment's performance on your overall portfolio. By diversifying, you can potentially lower the risk associated with investing in a single asset or sector. For example, if one industry or asset class experiences a downturn, other investments in your portfolio may help offset the losses.

2. **Benefits of Diversification**:
   - **Risk Reduction**: Diversification helps reduce the risk of significant losses by not relying heavily on a single investment. It can help protect your portfolio from the unpredictable nature of individual stocks or sectors.
   - **Smoothing Returns**: Diversification can help smooth out the volatility of your portfolio. When some investments are performing poorly, others may be performing well, thus balancing out overall returns.
   - **Capital Preservation**: Diversifying your investments can help preserve your capital by minimizing the impact of a single investment's poor performance on your overall portfolio.

3. **Risk Management**: Risk management involves identifying, assessing, and mitigating potential risks associated with investments. Here are some key risk management strategies:

12

- **Asset Allocation**: Determine the optimal mix of asset classes in your portfolio based on your risk tolerance, investment goals, and time horizon. By diversifying across different asset classes, you can manage risk effectively.

- **Portfolio Rebalancing**: Regularly review and rebalance your portfolio to maintain the desired asset allocation. Rebalancing involves selling assets that have performed well and buying those that have underperformed, ensuring that your portfolio remains aligned with your risk tolerance and investment objectives.

- **Risk Assessment**: Evaluate the risk associated with individual investments and consider factors such as market risk, liquidity risk, credit risk, and geopolitical risk. Understanding the risks involved can help you make informed investment decisions.

- **Stop-loss Orders**: Consider implementing stop-loss orders, which automatically sell a security if it reaches a predetermined price. This can help limit potential losses in case of a significant market downturn.

- **Regular Monitoring**: Stay vigilant and regularly monitor your investments. Keep track of market trends, company news, and economic indicators that may impact your portfolio. By staying informed, you can make timely adjustments to manage risk effectively.

Remember, while diversification and risk management can help reduce risk, they do not guarantee profit or completely eliminate the possibility of losses. It's important to assess your risk tolerance, seek professional advice, and diversify your investments based on your individual circumstances and investment goals.

5.**Chapter4:The Entrepreneurial Leap**

- Starting your own business venture.

Starting your own business venture can be an exciting and rewarding journey. Here are some key steps to consider when embarking on this path:

1. **Identify Your Business Idea**: Start by identifying a business idea that aligns with your passions, skills, and market demand. Conduct market research to assess the viability of your idea and understand your target audience.

2. **Create a Business Plan**: Develop a comprehensive business plan that outlines your goals, target market, competition, marketing strategies, financial projections, and operational details. A well-thought-out business plan will serve as a roadmap for your venture and help you secure funding if needed.

3. **Secure Financing**: Determine the financial requirements of your business and explore funding options such as personal savings, loans, grants, or seeking investors. Develop a financial plan that includes startup costs, operating expenses, and contingency funds.

4. **Legal and Regulatory Considerations**: Research and comply with the legal and regulatory requirements for starting a business in your industry and location. Register your business, obtain necessary licenses and permits, and ensure you have a solid understanding of tax obligations.

5. **Build a Support Network**: Surround yourself with mentors, advisors, and a network of like-minded entrepreneurs. Join entrepreneurial organizations, attend networking events, and seek guidance from experienced professionals who can provide valuable insights and support.

6. **Develop a Marketing Strategy**: Create a marketing plan to promote your products or services. Identify your target audience, develop a strong brand identity, create a compelling online presence, and explore various marketing channels such as social media, content marketing, and advertising.

7. **Build a Team**: Determine the skills and expertise you need to run your business effectively. Hire employees or consider outsourcing certain tasks to contractors or freelancers. Build a team that shares your vision and values, and empower them to contribute to the success of your venture.

8. **Manage Finances**: Establish a system to track and manage your finances. This includes setting up accounting processes, monitoring cash flow, and regularly reviewing financial statements. Consider using accounting software or consulting with a financial professional to ensure accurate bookkeeping and financial management.

9. **Adapt and Innovate**: Stay agile and be prepared to adapt your business strategies based on market feedback and changing trends. Continuously seek opportunities for innovation, improve your products or services, and stay ahead of your competition.

10. **Seek Continuous Learning**: Invest in your personal and professional development by staying updated on industry trends, attending workshops or seminars, and seeking feedback from customers and mentors. Embrace a growth mindset and be open to learning from both successes and failures.

Remember, starting a business requires dedication, perseverance, and a willingness to take calculated risks. It's important to be prepared for challenges and setbacks along the way. By following these steps and staying focused on your goals, you can increase your chances of building a successful business venture.

- Identifying profitable business ideas.

Identifying profitable business ideas requires a combination of market research, understanding consumer needs, and recognizing opportunities for innovation. Here are some strategies to help you identify potentially profitable business ideas:

1. **Follow your passions and interests**: Start by reflecting on your own passions, interests, and skills. Look for business ideas that align with your expertise and that you are passionate about. This will not only make your work more fulfilling but also increase your chances of success.

2. **Identify market gaps and needs**: Conduct market research to identify gaps or unmet needs in the market. Look for areas where there is a demand but few competitors. Talk to potential customers, research industry trends, and analyze market data to identify opportunities for new products or services.

3. **Observe consumer trends**: Stay up to date with consumer trends and changing preferences. Monitor social media, read industry publications, and engage with your target audience to understand their evolving needs and desires. Look for ways to create innovative solutions or improve existing products or services.

4. **Solve problems**: Consider business ideas that solve specific problems or pain points for consumers. Look for areas where people are experiencing difficulties or inefficiencies and find ways to provide a solution. This could involve improving existing products or services or introducing something entirely new.

5. **Explore emerging industries**: Keep an eye on emerging industries or technologies that have the potential for growth. Look for industries that are experiencing significant changes or disruptions and consider how you can leverage these trends to create a profitable business.

6. **Consider scalability and profitability**: Evaluate the scalability and profitability potential of your business ideas. Look for ideas that have the potential to grow and generate sustainable profits in the long term. Consider factors such as the size of the target market, profit margins, and the ability to scale operations.

7. **Assess your resources and capabilities**: Take an honest assessment of your available resources, skills, and capabilities. Consider how well-suited you are to execute the business idea and whether you have the necessary resources or can acquire them. This includes financial resources, expertise, networks, and access to suppliers or distribution channels.

8. **Validate your idea**: Once you have identified a potential business idea, validate it by conducting further market research and testing. Seek feedback from potential customers, conduct surveys or focus groups, and create prototypes or minimum viable products to gather feedback and refine your idea.

Remember, profitability is not guaranteed, and every business idea comes with risks. It's important to thoroughly research and evaluate each idea before committing to it. Additionally, having a solid business plan, understanding your target market, and implementing effective marketing strategies are crucial for turning a profitable idea into a successful business.

- Creating a business plan and sourcing funds.

Creating a business plan and sourcing funds are essential steps in launching a new business. Here's a guide to help you with both processes:

1. **Business Plan**:
   - **Executive Summary**: Provide an overview of your business, including the mission, vision, and key highlights.
   - **Company Description**: Describe your business concept, target market, and competitive advantage.
   - **Market Analysis**: Conduct market research to understand industry trends, target market demographics, and competitors.
   - **Products or Services**: Explain what you will offer, how it addresses customer needs, and any unique features or benefits.
   - **Marketing and Sales Strategy**: Outline your marketing plan, pricing strategy, distribution channels, and sales approach.
   - **Organization and Management**: Detail the structure of your business, key team members, and their roles and responsibilities.

- **Financial Projections**: Provide a financial forecast, including revenue projections, expenses, and break-even analysis.
- **Funding Request**: Specify the amount of funding you require and how it will be used.
- **Appendix**: Include any supporting documents, such as market research data, resumes of key team members, and legal documents.

2. **Sourcing Funds**:
- **Personal Savings**: Utilize your own savings to fund your business. This shows commitment and reduces reliance on external funding.
- **Friends and Family**: Seek investments or loans from friends and family who believe in your business idea.
- **Small Business Loans**: Research and apply for small business loans from banks, credit unions, or government-backed loan programs.
- **Venture Capitalists and Angel Investors**: Pitch your business idea to investors who provide funding in exchange for equity or ownership stakes.
- **Crowdfunding**: Create a compelling campaign on crowdfunding platforms to raise funds from a large number of people.
- **Grants and Competitions**: Explore grants or business competitions that provide funding to startups in specific industries or niches.
- **Partnerships and Sponsorships**: Seek strategic partnerships or sponsorships with established companies that can provide financial support or resources.

Remember to tailor your approach to the specific requirements of your business and industry. Additionally, be prepared to present a strong business case, demonstrate your expertise, and highlight the potential profitability and growth prospects of your venture. Finally, keep in mind that financial management and accountability are crucial, so ensure you have a plan to track and manage your funds effectively.

6. **Chapter 5: Mastering the Art of Negotiation**

- Enhancing your negotiation skills for better deals.

Enhancing your negotiation skills can help you secure better deals and maximize value in various situations. Here are some tips to improve your negotiation skills:

1. **Prepare Thoroughly**: Before entering a negotiation, gather as much information as possible about the other party, their needs, and any relevant market conditions. Understand your own goals, desired outcomes, and alternative options.

2. **Define Your Objectives**: Clearly identify your objectives and prioritize them. Determine the minimum acceptable outcome (BATNA - Best Alternative to a Negotiated Agreement) and the ideal outcome (target).

3. **Active Listening**: Listen actively to the other party's needs, concerns, and perspectives. Pay attention to both verbal and non-verbal cues to understand their underlying interests and motivations.

4. **Ask Open-ended Questions**: Use open-ended questions to gather more information and encourage the other party to share their thoughts and preferences. This helps build rapport and a deeper understanding of their needs.

5. **Build Rapport and Empathy**: Establishing rapport and showing empathy can create a positive atmosphere and foster trust. Find common ground and demonstrate that you understand and respect the other party's point of view.

6. **Create Win-Win Solutions**: Aim for mutually beneficial outcomes where both parties feel they have gained value. Look for creative solutions that address the interests of both parties and explore options beyond price or financial terms.

7. **Effective Communication**: Clearly articulate your thoughts, needs, and expectations. Use persuasive language, logical reasoning, and evidence to support your arguments. Be assertive but respectful, and avoid aggressive or confrontational behavior.

8. **Negotiate Multiple Issues Simultaneously**: Consider negotiating multiple issues simultaneously rather than focusing solely on price. This allows for trade-offs and compromises across different aspects of the deal, such as delivery terms, payment terms, or additional services.

9. **Manage Emotions**: Keep emotions in check and maintain a calm and composed demeanor. Emotional intelligence is crucial in understanding and managing your own emotions and those of the other party.

10. **Be Flexible and Creative**: Be open to alternative solutions and be willing to explore different options. Sometimes, a creative approach can lead to unexpected win-win outcomes.

11. **Negotiate Long-term Relationships**: Consider the long-term implications of the negotiation. Building and maintaining strong relationships can lead to future opportunities and more favorable deals.

12. **Continuously Learn and Improve**: Reflect on your negotiation experiences, analyze what worked well and what could be improved. Seek feedback and learn from others who excel in negotiation skills.

Remember, negotiation is a skill that can be developed and refined over time. Practice these techniques, adapt them to different situations, and always strive for a fair and mutually beneficial outcome.

- Case studies of successful negotiations.

Here are a few case studies of successful negotiations:

1. **Microsoft's Acquisition of LinkedIn**: In 2016, Microsoft successfully negotiated the acquisition of LinkedIn for $26.2 billion.

Microsoft recognized the value of LinkedIn's professional network and saw an opportunity to strengthen its position in the business software and services market. Through negotiations, Microsoft secured a deal that allowed LinkedIn to maintain its brand, culture, and independence while leveraging Microsoft's resources and technology.

2. **The Iran Nuclear Deal**: In 2015, the P5+1 countries (United States, China, Russia, United Kingdom, France, and Germany) successfully negotiated the Iran Nuclear Deal. The negotiations aimed to limit Iran's nuclear program in exchange for the lifting of economic sanctions. Through intense negotiations, the involved parties reached a comprehensive agreement that addressed the concerns of all parties involved and helped prevent the proliferation of nuclear weapons.

3. **NFL Players' Collective Bargaining Agreement**: In 2020, the National Football League (NFL) and the NFL Players Association (NFLPA) successfully negotiated a new Collective Bargaining Agreement (CBA). The negotiations involved various contentious issues, such as player compensation, revenue sharing, and player health and safety. Through effective negotiation and compromise, both parties reached an agreement that provided improved benefits for players, increased revenue sharing, and ensured the continued growth of the league.

4. **The Paris Climate Agreement**: In 2015, representatives from 196 countries successfully negotiated the Paris Climate Agreement. The negotiations aimed to address the global challenge of climate change by setting ambitious targets for reducing greenhouse gas emissions. Through lengthy and complex negotiations, the participating countries reached a historic agreement that set a framework for global cooperation in combating climate change.

5. **The Cuban Missile Crisis**: In 1962, the United States and the Soviet Union engaged in intense negotiations during the Cuban Missile Crisis. The negotiations aimed to resolve the standoff caused by the placement of Soviet missiles in Cuba. Through a combination of diplomatic negotiations, backchannel communications, and a

show of military strength, both parties reached a resolution that involved the removal of Soviet missiles from Cuba in exchange for a commitment by the United States not to invade Cuba.

These case studies highlight the importance of effective negotiation strategies, including thorough preparation, clear communication, collaboration, and the ability to find mutually beneficial solutions. Successful negotiations require a deep understanding of the interests and concerns of all parties involved, as well as the ability to navigate complex and challenging situations.

- Practical exercises and tips for effective negotiations.

Here are some practical exercises and tips for effective negotiations:

1. **Prepare and Research**: Before entering a negotiation, it's essential to gather as much information as possible about the other party, their interests, and their position. Research their background, previous negotiations, and any relevant market data. This knowledge will help you anticipate their needs, understand their perspective, and make informed decisions during the negotiation.

2. **Define Your Objectives**: Clearly define your objectives and desired outcomes for the negotiation. Determine your priorities and identify any potential trade-offs or concessions you are willing to make. This will help you stay focused and make strategic decisions during the negotiation process.

3. **Active Listening**: Practice active listening during negotiations. Pay close attention to what the other party is saying, ask clarifying questions, and seek to understand their underlying interests and concerns. This will help you build rapport, demonstrate empathy, and identify potential areas of collaboration or compromise.

4. **Build Relationships**: Building a rapport and establishing a positive relationship with the other party can contribute to successful negotiations. Find common ground, show respect, and maintain a professional and collaborative attitude. Building trust and goodwill

can lead to more productive discussions and increase the likelihood of reaching mutually beneficial agreements.

5. **Explore Win-Win Solutions**: Look for solutions that meet the needs and interests of both parties. Instead of focusing solely on your own position, try to understand the other party's perspective and identify potential areas of agreement. This collaborative approach can lead to creative solutions that benefit both parties and enhance the long-term relationship.

6. **Manage Emotions**: Keep emotions in check during negotiations. Stay calm, composed, and professional, even if faced with challenging or confrontational behavior. Emotional reactions can cloud judgment and hinder productive discussions. Take breaks if needed, and focus on the issues at hand rather than personal attacks.

7. **Be Flexible and Open to Compromise**: Negotiations often involve give-and-take. Be willing to explore alternative options and consider compromises that align with your objectives. Flexibility and a willingness to find common ground can help overcome impasses and facilitate successful outcomes.

8. **Practice Role-Playing**: Role-playing exercises can be valuable in honing negotiation skills. Take on different negotiation scenarios and play both sides of the negotiation to understand different perspectives and practice different strategies. This can help you anticipate potential challenges and develop effective responses.

9. **Seek Win-Win Alternatives**: If a negotiation reaches an impasse, consider exploring alternative solutions that can still benefit both parties. Brainstorm creative options, consider different variables or concessions, and think outside the box. This mindset can help break deadlocks and find mutually beneficial alternatives.

10. **Continuous Improvement**: After each negotiation, reflect on the process and outcomes. Identify areas for improvement and learn from both successes and failures. Keep refining your negotiation

skills through practice, seeking feedback, and staying updated on negotiation techniques and strategies.

Remember, effective negotiation is a skill that can be developed and refined over time. By incorporating these exercises and tips into your negotiation approach, you can enhance your ability to achieve successful outcomes and build strong, productive relationships.

7. **Chapter 6: Digital Domination - Making Money Online**

- Understanding the digital market.

Understanding the digital market is crucial in today's technology-driven world. Here are some key points to help you gain a deeper understanding:

1. **Digital Market Definition**: The digital market refers to the online ecosystem where businesses, consumers, and other stakeholders interact and engage in various activities, such as buying and selling products or services, conducting market research, advertising, and more. It encompasses websites, social media platforms, search engines, mobile apps, and other digital channels.

2. **Global Reach**: One of the significant advantages of the digital market is its global reach. It allows businesses to transcend geographical boundaries and target customers worldwide. This opens up opportunities for expansion and growth, regardless of physical location.

3. **E-commerce**: E-commerce plays a pivotal role in the digital market. It involves the buying and selling of products or services online. E-commerce platforms enable businesses to set up online stores, accept payments, and reach a wide customer base. Understanding e-commerce trends, consumer behavior, and effective marketing strategies is essential for success in the digital market.

4. **Digital Advertising**: Digital advertising is a key component of the digital market. It involves promoting products or services

through online channels, such as display ads, search engine marketing, social media advertising, influencer marketing, and more. Understanding different advertising platforms, targeting options, and analytics is crucial to optimize advertising efforts and reach the right audience.

5. **Data and Analytics**: The digital market generates vast amounts of data that can provide valuable insights for businesses. Analyzing customer behavior, preferences, and trends can help optimize marketing strategies, improve customer experience, and make data-driven decisions. Understanding data analytics tools and techniques is essential to harness the power of data in the digital market.

6. **Mobile Market**: With the proliferation of smartphones, the mobile market has become a significant aspect of the digital landscape. Mobile apps, mobile-optimized websites, and mobile advertising are essential for reaching and engaging with customers who primarily use mobile devices. Understanding mobile user behavior, mobile app development, and mobile marketing strategies is crucial for success in the digital market.

7. **Social Media**: Social media platforms have transformed the way businesses interact with customers and build relationships. Understanding the dynamics of different social media platforms, creating engaging content, and leveraging social media marketing techniques can help businesses effectively reach and connect with their target audience.

8. **Search Engine Optimization (SEO)**: SEO is the practice of optimizing websites and content to rank higher in search engine results. Understanding SEO techniques and best practices is crucial for businesses to improve their online visibility, drive organic traffic, and compete effectively in the digital market.

9. **Cybersecurity and Privacy**: As the digital market expands, the importance of cybersecurity and privacy increases. Businesses need to protect customer data, secure online transactions, and comply with data protection regulations. Understanding

cybersecurity threats, implementing robust security measures, and ensuring privacy compliance is vital to build trust and credibility in the digital market.

10. **Continuous Learning**: The digital market is constantly evolving, with new technologies, trends, and consumer behaviors emerging regularly. To stay ahead, it's important to continuously learn and adapt. Stay updated on the latest digital marketing strategies, technologies, and industry news through online resources, courses, webinars, and networking with industry professionals.

By understanding the dynamics of the digital market and staying abreast of its trends and developments, businesses can effectively navigate this landscape, connect with their target audience, and achieve their goals in the digital era.

   - Setting up online businesses such as e-commerce, dropshipping, affiliate marketing, etc.

Setting up an online business can be an exciting and rewarding venture. Here are some key points to consider when starting various types of online businesses:

1. **E-commerce**: E-commerce involves selling products or services online. To set up an e-commerce business, consider the following steps:

   - **Choose a product or niche**: Identify a product or niche that you want to sell online. Research market demand, competition, and target audience to ensure viability.
   - **Create an online store**: Set up an online store using e-commerce platforms like Shopify, WooCommerce, or BigCommerce. Customize the design, add product listings, and set up payment and shipping options.
   - **Marketing and promotion**: Develop a marketing strategy to drive traffic to your online store. Utilize digital marketing techniques such as social media marketing, search engine optimization (SEO), content marketing, and paid advertising to reach your target audience.

- **Order fulfillment**: Establish a reliable order fulfillment process, including inventory management, packaging, and shipping. Consider options like dropshipping (discussed below) or managing your own inventory.

2. **Dropshipping**: Dropshipping is a business model where you sell products without holding any inventory. Here's how to start a dropshipping business:

 - **Find a dropshipping supplier**: Research and identify reputable dropshipping suppliers that offer products you want to sell. Platforms like AliExpress and Oberlo can connect you with suppliers.
 - **Set up an online store**: Create an online store using e-commerce platforms like Shopify or WooCommerce. Import product listings from your chosen supplier and customize your store.
 - **Market your store**: Develop a marketing strategy to attract customers to your store. Utilize social media marketing, influencer marketing, and content marketing to promote your products.
 - **Order fulfillment**: When a customer places an order, forward the order details to the dropshipping supplier who will handle packaging and shipping directly to the customer.

3. **Affiliate Marketing**: Affiliate marketing involves promoting other people's products or services and earning a commission for each sale or lead generated. Here's how to get started:

 - **Choose a niche**: Select a niche that aligns with your interests and has a market demand. Research affiliate programs within that niche.
 - **Join affiliate programs**: Sign up for affiliate programs offered by companies within your chosen niche. Popular affiliate networks include Amazon Associates, ClickBank, and ShareASale.
 - **Promote affiliate products**: Create content (e.g., blog posts, videos) that promotes affiliate products. Include affiliate links in your content, and when a visitor makes a purchase through your link, you earn a commission.

- **Drive traffic**: Utilize various marketing channels like social media, SEO, email marketing, and content marketing to drive traffic to your affiliate links.

Remember, regardless of the type of online business you choose, it's essential to have a solid business plan, understand your target audience, and continuously analyze and optimize your strategies to ensure long-term success.

- Strategies for effective online marketing and branding.

Effective online marketing and branding are crucial for the success of any online business. Here are some strategies to consider:

1. **Define your target audience**: Understand your target audience's demographics, interests, and pain points. This knowledge will help you tailor your marketing messages and branding efforts to resonate with your ideal customers.

2. **Develop a strong brand identity**: Create a unique and consistent brand identity that reflects your business values and resonates with your target audience. This includes designing a memorable logo, selecting brand colors and fonts, and creating a brand voice that aligns with your business persona.

3. **Create a professional website**: Your website is the foundation of your online presence. Ensure it is visually appealing, user-friendly, and optimized for search engines. Include clear navigation, compelling content, and strong calls-to-action to drive conversions.

4. **Search Engine Optimization (SEO)**: Implement SEO strategies to improve your website's visibility in search engine results. Optimize your website's content, meta tags, and URLs for relevant keywords. Focus on creating high-quality, valuable content that attracts organic traffic.

5. **Content marketing**: Develop a content marketing strategy to engage and educate your audience. Create and share valuable content such as blog posts, videos, and infographics that align with your target audience's interests and needs. Promote your content through

social media, email marketing, and guest posting to increase brand visibility and drive traffic.

6. **Social media marketing**: Utilize social media platforms that align with your target audience to build brand awareness, engage with your audience, and drive traffic to your website. Create a content calendar, post regularly, and interact with your followers to build a loyal community.

7. **Influencer marketing**: Collaborate with influencers in your niche who have a significant following and influence. Partner with them to promote your products or services to their audience, increasing brand visibility and credibility.

8. **Email marketing**: Build an email list and utilize email marketing to nurture relationships with your audience. Send personalized and relevant emails, such as newsletters, product updates, and exclusive offers, to keep your subscribers engaged and drive conversions.

9. **Paid advertising**: Consider using paid advertising platforms like Google Ads, Facebook Ads, and Instagram Ads to reach a wider audience and drive targeted traffic to your website. Set clear goals, monitor your campaigns, and optimize them based on performance metrics.

10. **Monitor analytics and adjust strategies**: Regularly monitor website analytics, social media insights, and campaign performance to analyze the effectiveness of your marketing efforts. Make data-driven decisions and adjust your strategies accordingly to optimize results.

Remember, building a strong online presence takes time and consistent effort. Be patient, adapt to changes in the digital landscape, and continuously refine your marketing and branding strategies to stay ahead of the competition.

8. **Chapter 7: Real Estate - The Golden Goose**

- Introduction to real estate investment.

Real estate investment refers to the purchase, ownership, management, rental, or sale of real estate properties for the purpose of generating income or achieving long-term appreciation. It is a popular investment strategy that offers various opportunities for individuals and businesses to build wealth and diversify their investment portfolios.

Here are some key points to consider when exploring real estate investment:

1. **Types of Real Estate Investments**: Real estate investments can take different forms, including residential properties (such as houses, apartments, and vacation rentals), commercial properties (such as office buildings, retail spaces, and warehouses), industrial properties, and even land. Each type of investment has its own potential risks, returns, and market dynamics.

2. **Income Generation**: Real estate investments can generate income in different ways. Rental properties, for example, can provide a steady stream of rental income. Commercial properties may generate income through lease agreements with tenants. Additionally, real estate investments can appreciate in value over time, allowing for potential capital gains upon sale.

3. **Cash Flow and Return on Investment**: Cash flow is an important consideration in real estate investment. It refers to the income generated from the property after deducting expenses such as mortgage payments, property taxes, maintenance costs, and vacancy periods. Positive cash flow indicates that the property is generating more income than it costs to maintain, while negative cash flow means expenses exceed income. Return on investment (ROI) is another key metric to evaluate the profitability of a real estate investment.

4. **Market Analysis**: Before investing in real estate, it is crucial to conduct thorough market analysis. This involves researching

factors such as location, supply and demand dynamics, rental rates, property values, and economic indicators. Understanding the local market conditions will help you make informed investment decisions and identify areas with potential for growth and profitability.

5. **Financing Options**: Real estate investments often require substantial capital. Financing options include traditional bank loans, private lenders, partnerships, or even utilizing your own savings. It is important to carefully evaluate the financing options available and choose one that aligns with your investment goals and financial situation.

6. **Risk Management**: Like any investment, real estate carries inherent risks. These can include changes in market conditions, property damage, unexpected expenses, and tenant turnover. Proper risk management involves conducting due diligence, having contingency plans, obtaining insurance coverage, and maintaining a financial buffer for unforeseen circumstances.

7. **Property Management**: Depending on your investment strategy, you may choose to manage the property yourself or hire a professional property management company. Property management involves tasks such as tenant screening, rent collection, property maintenance, and handling legal and administrative responsibilities. Outsourcing property management can alleviate the workload and ensure the property is well-maintained.

8. **Tax Considerations**: Real estate investment has various tax implications. It is important to understand tax laws and regulations related to rental income, capital gains, property taxes, and deductions. Consult with a tax professional to optimize your tax strategy and maximize potential benefits.

9. **Long-Term Appreciation**: Real estate investments have the potential for long-term appreciation, meaning the value of the property may increase over time. Factors such as location, economic growth, infrastructure development, and market demand can contribute to property appreciation. However, it is important to note that property values can also fluctuate due to market conditions.

10. **Diversification**: Real estate investment can provide diversification to your investment portfolio. Real estate often behaves differently compared to other investment vehicles like stocks or bonds, which can provide a hedge against market volatility and potentially enhance overall portfolio stability.

Before embarking on a real estate investment journey, it is essential to educate yourself, seek advice from professionals, and conduct thorough research. Real estate investment can be lucrative, but it requires careful planning, analysis, and ongoing management to achieve success.

 - Strategies for buying, selling, and renting properties.

When it comes to buying, selling, and renting properties, there are various strategies you can employ to maximize your returns and achieve your investment goals. Here are some common strategies for each of these areas:

1. **Buying Properties**:
   - **Buy and Hold**: This strategy involves purchasing properties with the intention of holding onto them for an extended period. The goal is to generate rental income and benefit from long-term appreciation.
   - **Fix and Flip**: This strategy involves purchasing properties that need renovation or repairs, improving them, and then quickly selling them for a profit. It requires a keen eye for identifying undervalued properties and good project management skills.
   - **Wholesaling**: Wholesaling involves finding distressed properties at a low price and then assigning the purchase contract to another investor for a fee. This strategy requires strong negotiation skills and a network of potential buyers.
   - **Real Estate Investment Trusts (REITs)**: REITs are investment vehicles that allow you to invest in real estate without directly owning properties. REITs pool funds from multiple investors to purchase and manage income-generating properties.

2. **Selling Properties**:

- **Traditional Sale**: This is the most common method of selling properties. It involves listing the property on the market, marketing it to potential buyers, negotiating offers, and closing the sale.
- **Off-Market Sale**: Sometimes, properties are sold without being listed on the open market. This strategy involves networking with investors, real estate agents, and other industry professionals to find potential buyers.
- **Seller Financing**: In this strategy, the seller acts as the lender and provides financing to the buyer. This can attract more buyers, especially those who may have difficulty obtaining traditional financing.

3. **Renting Properties**:
- **Long-Term Rentals**: Renting out properties on a long-term basis is a common strategy for generating consistent rental income. It involves finding reliable tenants, conducting thorough background checks, and signing lease agreements.
- **Short-Term Rentals**: This strategy involves renting out properties on a short-term basis, typically through platforms like Airbnb or VRBO. Short-term rentals can generate higher rental income but require more active management.
- **Vacation Rentals**: Renting out properties in popular vacation destinations can be a lucrative strategy. It requires understanding the local tourism market, marketing the property effectively, and providing a memorable guest experience.

Regardless of the strategy you choose, it is important to conduct proper research, analyze market conditions, and consider factors such as location, property condition, financing options, and potential risks. It can also be beneficial to seek advice from real estate professionals, such as real estate agents, property managers, and investment advisors, to help you navigate the buying, selling, and renting process.

- Case studies of successful real estate investments.

Here are a few case studies of successful real estate investments:

1. **Warren Buffett's Investment in Laguna Beach Property**:

Warren Buffett, one of the most successful investors, purchased a beachfront property in Laguna Beach, California, in 1971 for $150,000. Over the years, the property's value increased significantly, and Buffett sold it in 2005 for a staggering $5 million. This investment showcased the power of long-term appreciation and the importance of investing in desirable locations.

2. **Donald Trump's Renovation of the Commodore Hotel**:
In the late 1970s, Donald Trump, the former U.S. president, acquired the Commodore Hotel in New York City. He transformed the aging hotel into the luxurious Grand Hyatt Hotel through a $100 million renovation project. The successful repositioning of the property not only increased its value but also revitalized the surrounding area, leading to further economic development.

3. **Sam Zell's Investment in Manufactured Housing**:
Sam Zell, a renowned real estate investor, recognized the potential in the manufactured housing sector. In the late 1990s, he acquired a major stake in Equity LifeStyle Properties (ELS), a real estate investment trust (REIT) specializing in manufactured home communities. Zell's investment paid off as the demand for affordable housing increased, and ELS experienced significant growth, providing consistent rental income and capital appreciation.

4. **Blackstone Group's Investment in Single-Family Homes**:
In the aftermath of the 2008 financial crisis, Blackstone Group, a global investment firm, recognized an opportunity in the distressed single-family home market. They purchased thousands of foreclosed properties at discounted prices and converted them into rental properties. Blackstone's strategic acquisition and management of these properties resulted in substantial returns, demonstrating the potential of the rental market during a recovery period.

These case studies highlight the importance of factors such as location, renovation and repositioning, market timing, and identifying emerging trends in real estate. Successful investors often combine thorough research, strategic decision-making, and a long-term perspective to achieve exceptional results. It's important to note that real estate investments come with risks, and it's crucial to conduct your own due diligence and seek professional advice before making any investment decisions.

Dear Reader,

I want to take a moment to express my sincerest gratitude for choosing to read my book. Your decision to invest your time and attention in exploring the pages of this book is deeply appreciated. Thank you for being a part of this journey with me.

Writing this book has been a labor of love, and I am grateful for the opportunity to share my knowledge and experiences with you. It is my hope that the words within these pages have provided you with valuable insights, inspiration, and practical guidance.

As an author, I understand the importance of honest feedback and reviews. Your opinion matters to me, and I would be immensely grateful if you could take a few moments to share your thoughts and impressions of the book. Your feedback can help me improve as a writer and provide valuable insights to potential readers.

If you enjoyed the book and found it helpful, I would greatly appreciate it if you could leave a review on platforms like Amazon, Goodreads, or any other relevant platforms. Your positive review can make a significant impact on the book's visibility and reach, allowing more readers to benefit from its contents.

Similarly, if there were aspects of the book that you feel could be improved or if you have any constructive criticism, I would be grateful to hear your thoughts. Your honest feedback will help me grow as an author and ensure that future editions or works better meet the needs of readers like yourself.

Once again, thank you for being a reader of this book. Your support and engagement mean the world to me. I am truly honored to have had the opportunity to share this journey with you, and I look forward to hearing your thoughts and insights.

With heartfelt appreciation,

M Livingston

www.ingramcontent.com/pod-product-compliance
Lightning Source LLC
Chambersburg PA
CBHW071218290526
45796CB00008B/285